Leading Lady

RAISA GORBACHEV

By Jill C. Wheeler

Published by Abdo & Daughters, 6535 Cecilia Circle, Edina, Minnesota 55439.

Library bound edition distributed by Rockbottom Books, Pentagon Tower, P.O. Box 36036, Minneapolis, Minnesota 55435.

Printed in the United States.

Cover Photo: Archive Photos
Inside Photos: Bettmann Newsphoto 5, 13, 22, 23, 27 & 31
Globe 8, 10, 20, 25 & 29

Edited by Rosemary Wallner

LIBRARY OF CONGRESS CATALOGING-IN-PUBLICATION DATA

Wheeler, Jill C., 1964-
Raisa Gorbachev / written by Jill C. Wheeler.
p. cm. — (Leading Ladies)
Summary: Presents the life of the wife of the man who led the Communist party in the USSR from 1985 to 1991.
ISBN 1-56239-118-6
1. Gorbachev, Raisa Maksimovna, 1932- --Juvenile literature. 2. Heads of state -- Soviet Union -- Wives -- Biography -- Juvenile literature. 3. Soviet Union -- Politics and government -- 1985-1991 -- Juvenile literature. (1. Gorbachev, Raisa Maksimovna, 1932- . 2. Heads of state -- Wives.] I. Title. II. Series.
DK290.3.G675W48 1992 947.085'4'092--dc20 92-16678
[B]

International Standard Book Number:
1-56239-118-6

Library of Congress Catalog Card Number:
92-16678

TABLE OF CONTENTS

FIRST LADY OF THE SOVIET UNION

Many Americans were curious when Soviet leader Mikhail Gorbachev first visited the United States. It was December 1987. Everyone wanted to glimpse the man who made history when he increased the freedoms in his country.

Some people were even more curious about the woman at his side. Soviet leaders' wives have never been in the public eye like the wives of United States presidents. Soviet newspapers often did not even mention leaders' wives. Some Soviets did not even know whether or not their leaders were married.

This Soviet First Lady was different. She was intelligent and well educated. She had beautiful red hair and a trim figure. Her clothing was fashionable. She enjoyed shopping and had a credit card. She was different from the image most Americans had of a Soviet woman.

Former Soviet leader Mikhail Gorbachev and his wife, Raisa.

Raisa has captured global attention ever since 1985. That year her husband became the leader of the Communist party that rules the Union of Soviet Socialist Republics (U.S.S.R.). She was his partner in making many of the reforms that changed the lives of the Soviet people. She supported her husband during difficult times.

"I am the wife of the head of the Soviet state," she said. "I support my husband as far as I can. In our family...the problem of each family member is everybody's problem."

A RAILWAY WORKER'S DAUGHTER

On a cold January day in 1932, a Siberian railway worker and his wife became parents of a baby girl. Maxim Titorenko and Shura Paradina named their daughter Raisa Maximovna Titorenko. Her parents shortened the name to Raya. Many Soviet people use nicknames all their lives.

Despite the harsh cold in her hometown, baby Raisa grew strong and healthy. She spent time with her grandparents while her mother worked as a railway inspector.

Her father's job often took him out of town. Even when Maxim was home, he frequently worked twelve-hour days.

Raisa's family considered themselves lucky. Maxim worked for the railway. People respected railway workers. Railway workers were paid better than many other laborers. They had uniforms to wear. They also had to move when the government told them.

When Raisa was two, her brother Evgeny was born. The same year her family moved 1,800 miles away to the Ukraine. Shura was sad to leave her parents and her hometown. She knew the family had no choice if Maxim wanted to keep his job.

LIVING WITH FEAR AND POVERTY

Raisa grew up in a dark period in Soviet history. Joseph Stalin ruled the country. Stalin would imprison or kill people who disagreed with him. He employed secret police to find out who spoke out against him. One day, those police heard Maxim disagree with Stalin's plans for farmers.

Joseph Stalin

Stalin wanted all farmers to work for the government. The police arrested Maxim and sent him to a labor camp. Raisa was three years old.

After Maxim's arrest, the police forced Shura and her children from their home. They had to move to a smaller house that had no electricity or running water. The family had little money. It took all of Shura's courage and strength to feed and clothe her children and keep them warm. She had no help. She could not visit her parents, either. Families of prisoners were not allowed to travel.

Despite such troubles, Shura worked to see that her children were happy. "She sang little songs, she was there, and we felt protected," Raisa said of her mother. "We used to go mushrooming. Our mother really watched over us."

After four years, the police released Maxim from the labor camp. The same year, Raisa began school and the world went to war. The Titorenko family moved many times. This was because the railway system would be critical if Russia joined the war. Their home was a railway wagon that they could hitch to a train. It could be moved easily. Raisa and her brother often changed schools. They met new teachers and new classmates.

SCHOOL DAYS

Raisa enjoyed school. Like all Russian children, she attended primary school for four years. The first two years, boys and girls studied together. After that, boys and girls were separated. All children learned math, the Russian language, physical education and art. Raisa liked literature and language the best.

World War II was a very trying time for Russia.

After school, Raisa watched her brother and her new baby sister, Ludmilla. Raisa also helped her mother. Her mother worked all day and took care of her family at night. Raisa's help became even more important in 1941. That year, World War II spread to Russia. Russian leaders asked the people to work longer and harder.

Raisa spent many hours studying and helping at home. She also belonged to the Young Pioneers. The Young Pioneers was a youth group that taught members about communism. Communism was the Russian form of government. With communism, a central government controls everything. Every morning, Raisa and her classmates took the Young Pioneers' pledge. They vowed to help with Stalin's plans for the country.

Raisa entered secondary school at age 11. She was an outstanding student. She took classes in history, geography, science, foreign languages and psychology. She and her classmates wore uniforms. They were not allowed to wear make-up. They never questioned when pictures in their textbooks were blotted out. In those days, people who Stalin disliked were removed from history books. Teachers were told to pretend those people never had lived.

Raisa was thirteen years old when World War II ended. The war had wracked her country. Nearly 20 million Russians had died, including many women and children. "Millions of lives lost, millions of lives ruined," Raisa said of the war. "Houses laid waste, families orphaned, towns and villages destroyed... . I remember it to this very day."

The Titorenko family's life slowly improved after the war. Raisa continued to excel in school. She graduated at the top of her class and earned the gold medal. Only one in one hundred students received the gold medal. The medal entitled Raisa to attend a university.

STUDYING AT MOSCOW UNIVERSITY

Raisa decided to study psychology at Moscow University. She wanted to enjoy the cultural life of Moscow. The city had theaters, music halls and art museums. It was a very different place from the small towns where she had lived.

The Kremlin, inside the city of Moscow, Russia.

Life as a student was not comfortable. Raisa lived in a fixed-up military barracks called a hostel. She shared a room with eleven other students. She had her own bed, but she shared all her other furniture. She kept her clothes and books in a box under her bed. The government gave Raisa and her fellow students a small allowance.

Because the hostels were so crowded, students often studied in the library. Studying was a privilege. Not all Russians could attend a university. Raisa took her classes seriously and did well. The government gave her more grant money because of her good grades.

Raisa used the money to take part in Moscow's culture. She also shed her country ways. She cut her long red hair, which she had worn in braids pinned on her head.

She bought nicer clothes. Her beauty caught the eye of many other university students. Among them was the son of an Ukrainian farmer who would one day lead his nation.

MEETING MIKHAIL GORBACHEV

Raisa tried new activities whenever she had time. Once, she took a rhythmic gymnastics class with a friend. In 1951, she took a dancing class. There she met a young man who had attended to poke fun at his friends. Raisa and the man, Mikhail Gorbachev, got along well. "We realized our life would be unthinkable without each other," Raisa recalled. "Our feelings were our very life itself."

Mikhail and Raisa dated for a year. They took walks in Moscow parks. They attended concerts, dances and the theater. Raisa accepted his proposal of marriage against both their parents' wishes. Their parents wanted them to finish school first.

The two married in fall 1953. After the civil ceremony, they celebrated with their fellow students. None of the family members attended.

Their honeymoon was one night alone in Mikhail's dorm room. After that, they returned to separate rooms. One year later, they were able to move in together. Student marriages were difficult at the university.

Raisa finished her degree before her husband. Her grades were so high she was offered a research fellowship. She could not pursue her fellowship, though. When Mikhail graduated in 1955, the government sent him to work in Stavropol (Stav-'raw-pul). Raisa put her plans – and her love of Moscow – on hold. She followed her husband.

ON TO STAVROPOL

Stavropol was a big change from Moscow for the Gorbachevs. The city had only 100,000 residents. Most of the people were farmers. There were few theaters and museums. But Stavropol did not have long, cold winters like Moscow did.

The Gorbachevs lived a simple life in Stavropol. Their living quarters were small. They had no bathroom. Mikhail's job was with the Communist party. Raisa taught at the Stavropol Agricultural Institute. Like most Russians, they did not complain about their jobs.

Shortly after they moved, Mikhail was promoted. With his promotion, he and Raisa became members of the Communist party's elite.

As members of the elite, the Gorbachevs received a car and a nicer apartment. They had access to the best food and clothing and the finest wines. Raisa enjoyed their new comforts. She also became a mother. On January 6, 1958, her daughter Irina Mikhailovna was born.

Motherhood changed Raisa. She became less shy. She enjoyed helping Mikhail entertain guests visiting the local hot springs. Many of these guests were top Communist officials. This gave Mikhail and Raisa the chance to meet many of the men who ran the country. Many of the men took notice of Mikhail as well.

DR. GORBACHEV

Raisa resumed her education several years after moving to Stavropol. She decided to study sociology. She began a research paper to earn her doctoral degree. She studied the economic and social conditions of the local farmers.

Raisa's studies became a help to her husband. Her research showed farmers produced more when they had more education. She also said the peasants needed more culture. Mikhail followed Raisa's advice. The government praised him for his work in increasing the local food supply.

Stavropol had no university with a sociology program. Raisa applied for the program at the Lenin Pedagogical Institute in Moscow. In 1964, the school accepted her. Now she traveled to Moscow several times a year. There she reviewed the results of her research with her teachers.

By 1967, Raisa had passed all her exams. Her teachers accepted her paper on the Stavropol peasants. She now could be called Dr. Gorbachev. She became the first Communist party official's wife to write a doctoral paper.

CLIMBING THE LADDER

As Raisa worked toward her degree, her husband worked toward more promotions. He had reached the highest rank possible outside of Moscow in 1970.

He was in charge of the Communist party's activities in the entire Stavropol region. (Stavropol is about the size of South Carolina.)

Mikhail's accomplishments pleased Raisa. For fifteen years, she had worked with him like a partner. She had read books and briefed him on what she had learned. She helped him cultivate an interest in the arts. She did an excellent job as a government official's wife.

Raisa believed her husband soon would win more responsibility. In November 1978, Mikhail was appointed to the Soviet Central Committee. The family returned to Moscow. By the end of 1980, Mikhail was a full member of the country's ruling Politburo. In March 1985, he succeeded Konstantin Chernenko. He was now the General Secretary of the Communist party.

Mikhail Gorbachev addressing the Politburo.

Raisa remembered his concerns about the new position. "It is impossible to achieve anything on a large scale," Mikhail said. "...Yet life demands it... . We just can't go on like this."

LEADER AT LAST

With her husband now his country's leader, Raisa's life changed. The family moved to a large house on a tree-lined avenue. They enjoyed gourmet food and designer clothing. They had a full staff of household help. Wherever they went, limousines accompanied them. Raisa had a chauffeur to drive her around, too. Like most Soviet women, she does not have a driver's license.

Raisa and Mikhail also traveled more. Raisa accompanied her husband on his trips around the world. Former Soviet leaders had kept their wives in the background. But Mikhail took pride in having his wife at his side. On her first visit to the United States, Raisa charmed news reporters. They warmed to her ready smile, intelligence and curiosity.

Mikhail Gorbachev and wife Raisa visit the Great Wall of China.

Part of Raisa's appeal was her husband's work. Mikhail was making history through a program of economic and political reforms. These reforms were called perestroika (pe-re-'stroy-kah). That is the Russian word for restructuring.

Mikhail believed the Soviet people needed freedom to improve their lives. He wanted the Communist party to have less control. He wanted elections with more than one candidate. He wanted less government control over what the newspapers printed.

Moscow, March 17, 1991- Raisa Gorbachev casts her vote for the future leader of her country.

Mikhail's ideas angered many people in his country. Some believed communism should not allow such freedoms. Others wanted the freedom. But they became upset when perestroika led to labor strikes and food shortages.

MAKING HISTORY

Under Mikhail, life changed in the Soviet Union. Life also changed in other Communist-controlled nations. In November 1989, the Berlin Wall came down. That wall had symbolized the separation of East Germany from West Germany. When the wall came down, Germany became one nation after nearly thirty years of being divided.

Many other nations that had been linked to the U.S.S.R. declared their independence. They set up new governments. Russian soldiers were ordered to leave Afghanistan.

They had been fighting for control there. In the U.S., people declared the Cold War was over. The Cold War was the name given to the poor relations between the U.S. and the Soviet Union.

The Berlin Wall, symbolizing a divided nation.

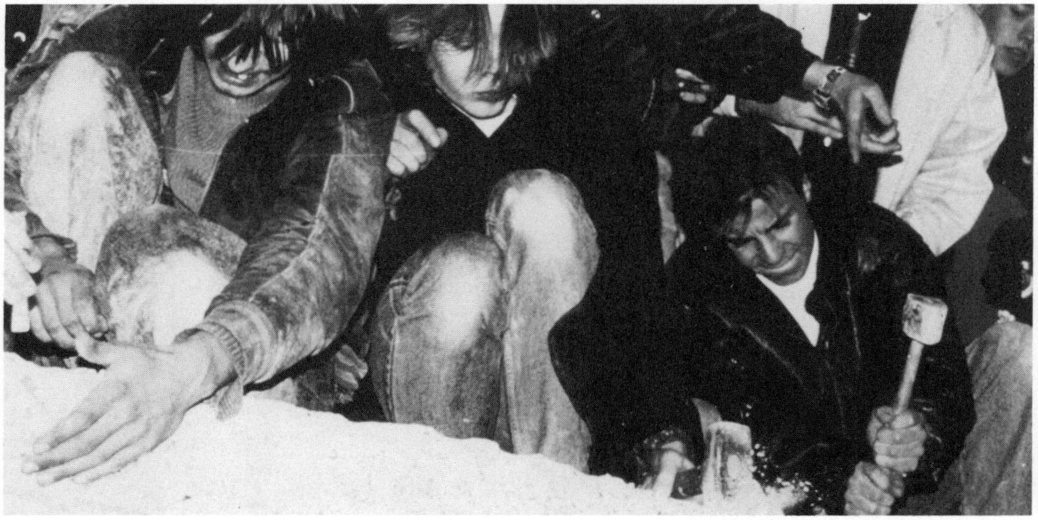

The Berlin Wall coming down.

People around the world hailed Mikhail as a hero. But in his own country, people often criticized him. Many Russians said their nation was falling apart. They wanted things to be the way they used to be. Mikhail realized there might be trouble ahead. In August 1990 he told Raisa, "We've got the most difficult time ahead of us."

TERROR IN AUGUST

Mikhail's predictions came true a year later. On the afternoon of August 18, 1991, Raisa's husband came to her at their home near the Black Sea. His face showed fear and concern. He told her a group of men from Moscow had come to see him. He had tried to use the telephone and found it was no longer working.

Soon, Mikhail's fears were realized. His enemies had plotted to remove him from power. They wanted to run the country. The men had planned a coup.
For three days, the men held the Gorbachevs prisoner. The world held its breath to see if Gorbachev's enemies would succeed. Many people feared the Gorbachev family had been killed.

The brutal forces of civil war destroyed this city.

Help for the Gorbachevs came from an unlikely source. Boris Yeltsin was the president of the Russian republic. He and Mikhail had disagreed on many things. But Boris Yeltsin stood up to Mikhail's enemies. He was able to stop them. He told the men to release the Gorbachevs and fly them back to Moscow.

The coup attempt accelerated the changes taking place in the Soviet government. Soon, Mikhail ordered the Communist party to be dissolved. In December 1991, leaders of Russia and ten other former Soviet republics made an announcement. They said they were forming a Commonwealth of Independent States. They said the Commonwealth would replace the Soviet Union.

Mikhail realized his job was finished. With no country to govern, he resigned on December 25, 1991. His dream of transforming his country had come true. But he had not realized how much that dream would cost everyone.

Boris Yeltsin, new leader of Russia.

AN UNCERTAIN FUTURE

The Gorbachevs now face an uncertain future. The Commonwealth struggles with food shortages and confusion. Communist demonstrators gather almost daily in Moscow to protest the new government. Around the world, people anxiously await the next chapter in Russian history.

The Gorbachevs also are watching events unfold. They have endured much in their thirty-nine years of marriage. Now they face the future with the strength that has served them well before.

"We have had everything in our life," Raisa said. "Joy and sorrow ... successes and failures, poverty, hunger... . He and I have gone through it all while still preserving...our devotion to our ideas and ideals.

"I believe that strength of spirit, courage and firmness will help my husband," added Raisa, "to withstand the unprecedented ordeals of the most difficult stage in our life."

The Gorbachevs saying goodbye.

INDEX: